# How To Take Control Of Your Life and Begin Living Without Worry

**Worry is a habit. Get rid of it -- Now and forever!**

The years have been kind to you but it certainly didn't have anything to do with what you were doing to help the cause. Each day you slipped out of bed your first thought was one of worrying about what you had to do, how you were going to do it and whether or not you would survive for just one more day. No, it wasn't because of you that is for certain. And then it happened: You learned how to leave worry behind, to break the destructive habit of constantly fearing life and you actually began to live life rather than just existing. You finally were able to leave the maddening crowd behind and live life on your terms. Congratulations!

**In this book you'll discover how to:**

*  Eliminate nearly all of those useless business and everyday life-sucking worries immediately.

*  Reduce financial worries and never look back.

*   Get so much sleep people won't recognize you because of your newfound enthusiasm for life. They'll say "You look so young!"

*  An hour a day will keep the doctor away. Walk it off and see just how good you'll feel.

*  Learn how to actually find yourself and be yourself -- There is no one else on earth like you!

Explore the fundamental changes you need to make in your emotions and life habits. No more will you have to fear life, worry about everything and be so filled with anxiety that you don't even want to leave your house. That ends now!

## What do you worry about?

If you haven't worried about anything this past week, then don't read this.

But, I'm guessing you have. Even the most enlightened and spiritual person will sometimes find themselves in a state of worry.

We worry about different things. We worry about our children, marriage, job, parents or money.

Your children worry just as much as you but over different things. (Even if they act like they don't care about anything)

They worry about their friends, or if they'll make the team or get in the college of their choice.

## Worry is an uninvited guest.

You don't wake up and think I will worry today. It hijacks you when you are driving, taking a shower or trying to get some work done. It comes unannounced and then it doesn't want to leave.

## Worry eats up all your attention.

It doesn't matter what you're doing or where you are, when you have a worry attack, it consumes all of your attention. That's why you can't focus and you end up preoccupied, scattered and in a big fog.

When worry takes over you make stupid mistakes, like going to the grocery store to buy milk and then you buy everything but the milk.

## Worry drains your "I feel good" energy.

Imagine your brain is a computer. Worry is like viruses and adware. When viruses attack your computer everything slows down and you are left staring at the spinning circle.

The same is with worry. You can't focus on the good things in life, because all your attention is eaten up by worry.

Your thoughts start spinning just like the spinning circle on the computer and your brain freezes up.

**Worry robs you of blessings and is contagious.**

5 Ways to turn worry around

## 1. Name the worry

Worry thoughts spin so fast in our brains it's hard to know what we are worrying about. These thoughts are like an old fashioned record that gets stuck and plays the same thing over and over again.

Take 5 minutes and write down what you are worrying about. Write everything about it. What are you afraid of now and in the future? How does your worry impact the people you love? Write it all out.

Though this feels counterintuitive this saves you time in the long run.

## 2. Let your worry plead its case

Give your worry time to plead its case. Here is the secret. Tell your worry I will listen to you one time, now give me your best shot. And then really go for it. Worry. Worry. Worry. Now you are done. You don't have to worry about this same thing 5 million more times.

## 3. Now it's time to cross examine your worry

After the worry has pleaded its case you are going to cross examine.

Ask your worry "is this really true?" The worry thought is going to say, "Yes it is true."

Then you can ask another question, "How likely will that happen?" Yes, bad things happen, but how likely is this going to happen to you? These questions help you take the mountain down to the molehill.

## 4. Take action

Now that you have a more realistic picture of what you are worrying about, ask yourself this question. "What action do I need to take?" "Is there something I can do to proactively deal with my worry. Decide what you are going to do and then let it go.

See, worry is about feeling out of control.

When you decide what you are going to do, the worry calms down because you have taken back the reins.

## 5. Look for the blessing

Is there a blessing behind your worry?

Ask yourself this question. How would your life be different if you spent one day worry free?

If it's one thing that I see in the lives of many people today, it's unnecessary worry. You see people worrying about a whole lot of nonsense. Worrying about what they're going to eat, worrying about how they're going to pay the bills, worrying about what's going on with the kids, worrying about the job, worrying about what they heard on CNN...just constant worry.

I've met people who were once professional worriers. They used to wake up worrying and go to bed worrying. The irony of it is that they didn't understand the magnitude of the problem they were causing when they continued to worry. And they failed to realize the consequences. You talk to the average person and they will try to convince you that nothing is wrong with worrying. They'll even say something like, "everybody does it". First of all, that's a lie. And secondly, you shouldn't come to the conclusion that something is OK, just because everybody supposedly does it.

It can be quite devastating to a person, if they never really understand how destructive worry can be for the worrier. Once they realize the negative impact of unnecessary worry, and understand that worry is a form of fear that should not be tolerated, the light bulb usually goes on. So if you're worrying about the economy, worrying if it's going to rain tomorrow, worrying if you offended someone at work today, worrying if you got a disease, worrying about what you saw on television, or read in the newspaper, worrying if you'll get laid off from your job, worrying if you'll have enough gas to get to work...if you are worrying about all of these type of things, then you've formed a bad habit that needs to be broken. Why? Because there is absolutely nothing good to be gained from useless worrying, and everything good and perfect to be gained from being happy.

## Negative Meditation

Worry is when you meditate on what's negative. Worry is fear based meditation. And the first step to overcoming fear is to recognize it. Worry is fear in disguise. It's when you deliberately and constantly think about something that has a negative result... always considering the worst outcome, and then, before you know it, you're consumed by non-stop worrying.

And when someone continues to worry, they'll soon find out that the things that they are worrying about the most, the very things that they fear the most, guess what? Without realizing it, they are now planning on it actually happening. It's like they're rehearsing their worst fears, over and over.

Just like a person can produce successful results in positive meditation, they can also produce the same kind of results in worrying. What happens is that, without warning, through persistent worry, a person now becomes an active participant in some type of tragedy that they've created through worry. They have no one to blame but themselves, because they helped create the disaster that's happened in their life, because they worried, and meditated on it every chance they had, day and night.

They should applaud themselves for laying down such a good foundation that was created for the sleepless nights they go through, the loneliness they feel, the depression they endure, their dreaded fears, the anxiety they experience... and all of the things that are going on in their life...they created it. When you worry, you are spending useless time thinking on the worst possible scenario. Worry is a form of fear that you must deal with, otherwise, it will deal with you.

## Guaranteed Results

When you find someone sitting at home constantly saying things like "Oh, my oh my, I'm so worried. Oooh, I'm worried about my job, I'm worried about the brakes on my car, I'm worried about my child, I'm so worried something going to happen to my child, I'm worried something bad is going to happen to my child". Then, this worrier finally gets the manifestation of what they kept worrying about, the very thing they have helped to bring to pass through their successful, constant worrying.

They get that 4 a.m. phone call that their child is in the hospital or in jail. And what's the first thing that this worrier will cry out? "Oooh Lord, I knew it!" Well yes, they should have known it. They meditated on it long enough for it to come to pass. So, why wouldn't it happen? But for some reason, what people don't realize is that worrying does create, what it creates, on the negative side. What they constantly worry about is created in reality, because worry is meditating on the wrong thing. And whatever a person meditates on over and over, the results are guaranteed.

Some of you reading this article are worried about something right now, worried how long it will take you to read this article, worried if the sun's going to shine tomorrow, just worried about nothing, worried about what someone thinks about you, worrying if you have enough money in bank. The worried mind endlessly keeps alive life's possible perils. Instead of coming up with creative solutions to potential problems, anxious thoughts keep the worried person stuck in an inflexible, relentless rut.

Worry is the most common form anxiety takes. Fearful, upsetting thoughts can become ruthless. Chronic worry has all the attributes of a low-grade emotional hijacking. The habit of worry becomes so ingrained that the anxious person can always find something to worry about, worry about lack, worry about social embarrassment, worry about your haircut, a fear of failure, rejection in love, family problems, on and on.

## The Profile of a Worrier

Have you ever met someone who's a real worrier? They're intense, sometimes extreme. You see it written all over their face. Just looking at them, you can tell that something is wrong. Ask them something like, "What's wrong with you today?" Before they reply, you'll see that their entire character is personalized with the traits of a worrier.

Look at the way their entire mouth is twisted to the side, their face crooked, they are usually slouched over, walking with a shuffle, and when they begin to speak, their words come out in a slow drawl, and they'll say something like, "You know, I just don't know, Oh, I'm just worried". And then you reply, "What are you worried about?" And the worrier will reply, "You know, it's always something".

## Concerned or Worried

A valuable distinction needs to be made between effective concern and useless worry. Your worry list may include many causes for genuine concern. If you eat a high-fat diet, smoke cigarettes and drink, and don't exercise, you are at greater risk for a heart attack: valid reasons for concern, right?

The difference between a valid concern and a useless worry lies in your ability to do something about the potential disasters that may lie ahead. Concern leads to action. Worry leads to potential destruction. If you're concerned about your health, do something about it. Make changes in your diet, begin a regular exercise regimen. Stop smoking and drinking alcohol. Concern is a natural expression of your ability to control your own destiny.

Worry is contrary to being concern. When you worry, your power to do something about potential problems never really enters into picture. You fail to come up with solutions. The opposite is the case, instead of coming up with solutions, you add more possible worst-case scenarios to the picture. Worry arises from feelings of powerlessness. When a person worries, for instance, they may speculate on all the problems their family will face if they lose their job. They always worry about something bad happening. The worrier is always in the mist of some type of disaster, helpless in doing something to solve the problem, while a concerned person is always seeking a way to create solutions.

Research has shown that being consumed with worry and being happy at the same time is hard to accomplish, because both cannot occupy the same space equally, one will overtake the other...it's your choice...choose to be happy. If you just look out a few minutes every morning, when you first wake up, and meditate on positive outcomes for the day instead of worrying, your brain reward you with happy, inspiring thoughts. This simple task can help you look and feel 10 years younger.

**Here's a quote I think you might like:**

"If we would keep filling our minds with the picture of happy things ahead, many worries and anxieties, and perhaps ill health, would naturally melt away. Always expect the best. Then if you have to hurdle a few tough problems, you will have generated the strength and courage to do so."

## WORRIES ARE A PLAIN NUISANCE!

They cause enormous stress affecting us both mentally and physically. If you've ever been lying awake worrying and unable to fall asleep, just to wake up with a sleep deficit the next morning you know what I mean.

## THE DIFFERENCE BETWEEN WORRIED AND HAPPY PEOPLE

Stressed people always have too many worries all rooted in one basic fear: the fear of not meeting expectations (whose expectations anyway? and how important are these people really?).

Happy people have worries, too, but the difference is that they know how to deal with them effectively and get rid of them fast. This article will make these tools available to you, too.

## WORRIES GROW WITH ATTENTION TO THEM

Most people cannot let go of their worrisome thoughts as if forgetting about them will make the dreaded thing happen. Guess what? The opposite is true. Worries grow the more attention you give them. The great news, however, is: you already have the power to make them go away. And this article will show you how to use it.

## WORRIES ARE THOUGHTS WHICH MAKE YOU FEEL BAD - REPLACE THEM

To reassure you straight away that it is possible, just make yourself aware of the fact that worries are nothing but thoughts which make you feel bad. Yes, worries are thoughts that derive from thinking about a possible negative outcome, an unwanted turn of events. Who chooses what you think? I hope your answer is: ME, or else we have a different issue to tackle. So if YOU decide what you think, then YOU are in control of what sort of thoughts you want to have, right? Once you become aware of this simple fact, you instantly know WHAT to do: replace the painful and unpleasant thoughts with more uplifting and energizing ones.

This leaves the question of the HOW to do that. After a few more important facts about worries, this article will show you several strategies on how to take control over your thoughts.

## WORRIES ARE USELESS - HERE IS PROOF

Worries are the anti-thesis to happiness. They distract you from enjoying life and the NOW - the only time to experience happiness. Here is why ALL worries are wasted:

40% of worries are about events that will never happen

30% of worries are about events that have already happened

22% of worries are about trivial events

4% of worries are about events we cannot change

4% of worries are about real events on which we can act
(and these are also wasted because we can actually do something about them)

## THE ROOT CAUSE OF ALL WORRIES

There is one underlying for all sorts of worries. It is the fear not to be able to handle the situation. That's it. Whatever you worry about, ultimately, you are afraid of not being able to handle the consequences. The truth is, however, you will always be able to find a way forward. That way forward may not be the one you had in mind before, but it will be there. Even if you don't know a way forward now, trust that you will figure it out when it all comes to it. TRUST is a key concept here. Just imagine, you would KNOW that whatever happens, whatever life throws at you, you will manage somehow, you will find some sort of way forward. If you knew that, what would there be left to fear? The answer is: NOTHING. And what if life always gave you exactly what you needed to make progress in your personal development? Then you could relax and let it come - whatever it is. Decide to trust: " Whatever happens, I will handle it" and notice how it makes you feel.

## FACT: THERE IS NO PROGRESS WITHOUT FEAR AND WORRIES

The fact is, as long as you develop fear and worries will ALWAYS be in your life. Yes! They will NEVER go away. Everytime you try something new, you step out of your comfort zone, and the uncertainty about the outcome will produce feelings of fear and worrisome thoughts. This is the same for everyone. Once you know that fear and worries will always be part of a meaningful and exciting life, you can relax and focus your energy on managing your worries rather than fighting them. The best way to manage fear and worries is to go ahead regardless of them and trust that you can handle whatever comes next. Make fear and worries your companion in life.

## 6 STRATEGIES TO DEAL WITH WORRIES:

## 1. USE LOGIC

Ask yourself what is really true about this fear or worry? Go and find the facts alone or with a partner. You will see that most worries are totally generalized, over-exaggerated or plain false! Thoughts like "nobody likes me" are rarely ever true and yet their devastating effect on your emotions is as real as if it was. So don't TRUST your worries! Once you have the facts (e.g. well, my mum likes me, my neighbour/doctor likes me etc. etc), the worry loses its power. There is a story about a man seeing a doctor.

The man said, "It's over. I'm finished. All my money has gone. I'VE LOST EVERYTHING."

Dr. asked, "Can you still see?"

The man replied, "Yes, I can still see."

Dr. asked, "Can you still walk?"

The man replied, "Yes, I can still walk."

Doctor said, "Obviously you can still hear of you wouldn't have phoned me."

"Yes, I can still hear."

"Well, I figure you have got about EVERYTHING LEFT. All you have lost is your money!"

We tend to generalize "lost everything" and feel the respective negative feelings, when in reality we (only) lost some/a lot of money.

## 2. REMIND YOURSELF, THAT BAD THINGS DON'T HAPPEN THAT OFTEN

We tend to expect the worst every time but the worst hardly ever happens. How often has the worst case scenario truly come to life for you? Rarely, I bet. So why do we insist that next time it will happen? It's simply a bad habit. So tell yourself, that the worst thing happens very rarely!

## 3. REMIND YOURSELF, THAT EVEN IF THINGS ARE A LITTLE BIT BAD, YOU CAN HANDLE IT AND GET THROUGH IT

So even if things don't work out the way you hoped. It's hardly ever the end of the world. Focus on the things you are still grateful for and try and see something positive in the outcome even if it's difficult to spot at first. I had cancer a couple of years ago and it felt like the end of the world at first, but it was also a blessing for me, a wake up call to re-focus on what truly matters to me, rather than blindly following the expectations of my boss/my company/society as a whole. If nothing else, you will always find some learning in a bad outcome - learning you would never have had, had it turned out otherwise! So look for the little good in the bad and keep going.

Next time you find yourself despairing, ask yourself these questions:

1.  Have I got enough air to breathe?

2. Have I got enough food for today?

3. Am I going to survive?

If the answer is YES, things are already looking up! So often, we magnify things out of proportion. The worst thing that could happen is probably very inconvenient, but not the end of the world.

If it helps you, make a plan of what you would do in the worst case scenario. This often helps to realize that things won't be all that bad after all and you will gain some valuable peace of mind.

## 4. IGNORE YOUR WORRIES

You already know that worries grow with attention. The opposite is true as well. When you don't spend time on them, worries shrivel and go away!

Obviously you cannot simply NOT worry at all but you can manage your worries. Set a specific worry time every day: 15 minutes in which you are allowed to worry about everything and anything. Just don't do it outside your worry time.

If your worry pops up outside worry time, either imagine a box in your mind in which you lock this worry till it's time or simply write it on a piece of paper and then put it away till worry time. You know you will spend time on it later.

Ask others to support you with this. Inform them about when your worry time is! Distract yourself with something else in the meantime. As if you switch a television channel, change thinking channel by remembering a happy memory, something that made you fell fabulous. Remember it with all your senses (what you see, hear, smell, felt, tasted). Alternatively think of something you are good at (comforting your child, folding clothes, skiing or coming up with ideas etc etc). Use this tool every time you need to, ideally 5 minutes daily.

At first this will feel hard, as you have so many worries and you can't wait to think or talk about them. After a while, however, something remarkable will happen...your list or your mental box won't be as full as you thought.

## 5. STAND UP TO YOUR WORRY & TALK BACK

Did you know that your worry is actually a bully? As long as you take it, the bully will continue to mistreat you. Imagine the bully as an ugly creature. Get angry and talk back.

At first the bully is still stronger than you (after all it had you under control for so long) but you can train to win this match. You already know that your worry bully generalizes, over-exaggerates and lies. He will try and make you believe that the worst thing will definitely happen when it is very unlikely to happen. So don't trust it! TALK BACK and imagine kicking or flicking it away. Keep doing that (the bully sees you as a weakling you listens to everything) as the bully will try again several times. Keep busy with something else.

## 6. STRENGTHEN YOUR BODY - RELAX AND EXERCISE

Research shows that good nutrition, regular exercise and sufficient 6-8 hours of sleep keep worries away. Without it, you literally invite the worries into your life.

### Worry A Little.  Live A Lot

As much as I wish I was perfect, I'm not. I worry.  Worry is not comfortable and I have always wished I knew how to worry less and how to be comfortable with whatever is going on. It's hard to change something I don't understand so I have put some thought and study into worry. Here's what I have come up with:

We worry about what we care about. So maybe worry shouldn't be completely eliminated from our lives. When we care about the safety of people we love, or the success or quality of what we are doing, or the viability of our business and livelihood, or anything else that is important to us, we feel at least a twinge of worry or concern. I'm not sure it's a good idea to completely get to a que sera, sera (whatever will be, will be) attitude. I have heard performers--even those who have done it for many decades--say that they haven't figured out how to overcome stage fright (worry) and don't completely want to get rid of it. It gives them an edge that makes them better. If they don't care, they aren't as good. I've known people who don't seem to care about anything and don't seem to worry or be concerned about anything. They're usually the people who will tell you that they don't give a %*#)! about things. Well I certainly don't want to be like them. So for those of you who, like me, worry a bit; well, it might be healthy, and maybe you shouldn't worry so much about worrying. Worrying won't change anything, but maybe it helps us realize and hone a little more what is important to us.

However, I have also been around people who seem to worry about everything and all the time. It's the only emotion they seem to have. It shows on their faces and in their lives. As with everything, too much of something is not good. Worrying all the time goes past caring about worthy things and goes to a lack of self-esteem and over-concern about what other people think, or unrealistic freaking out about what could possibly happen. Given the universe and eternity, just about everything will happen sooner or later, but we don't need to worry about 99.9999999999 percent of it, ever. I am not a psychologist or a psychiatrist and am not trained to solve mental problems. If someone worries so much that it is ruining their lives, they should probably see a psychologist or psychiatrist. The only thing I can offer is don't worry about yourself. You would not worry about what other people think of you if you realized how seldom they think of you. We are in control of ourselves. We should not worry about that; we should just get busy and control ourselves. We can be what we want to be, we can have, do, and give what we want. We don't need to worry about it. We just have to work for it.

Worry is creating mental pictures of what you don't want to happen. Confidence is creating mental pictures of what you do want to happen.

So if we can use worry to show us the difference between what is desirable and undesirable to us, we can then excuse worry, and we can work with confidence toward where we want to be. We can't let worry drive us because it will ruin our lives, but we can use a little bit of concern to drive ourselves to better things. Worry can never be allowed to cause us problems, it should be used to help us solve problems.

If we have too much worry in our lives, we should get busy doing something. Something related to what we're worried about, or even something not related. I have been worrying about something today. I'm trying to arrange something to where I can do some work and make some money. Instead of letting it get the best of me, I'm writing this article. Doing something, even though it is not related to what I'm worried about, gets my mind off of what I am worried about and helps me calm down. I also called someone else about the thing I'm most worried about, instead of waiting for a call that seemed overdue, and I found out some things that have helped relieve some of my worry.

I'm perfectly aware that in a day or two, the storm will have blown over, things will have happened the way they have happened and things will be the way they will be. The worry will be gone. There will be nothing left to worry about concerning this particular situation. It's good that working toward a resolution will push instances of worry out of our lives.

**Your Business Will Survive.  Give Yourself A Break:**

"In every life we have some trouble. When you worry you make it double. Don't worry. Be happy."

It seems like everyone is worrying these days.

It is not surprising with the current state of our economy.

Entrepreneurs worry about their businesses - online home businesses and brick and mortar businesses.

People worry about losing their jobs or house, paying bills, rising costs and the threat of rising taxes...and the list goes on.

Worrying is natural and easy, but are we becoming a nation of chronic worriers?

Do not get me wrong. Worry can be beneficial to us if it encourages us to change a troublesome situation. However, worrying is a problem when it leads to anxiety, fear and physical side effects like headaches, muscle tension and upset stomach.

If worry is affecting you this way...

Here are some tips so you don't worry for long

**1. Practice relaxing** - Relaxing has the opposite physical response in your body than anxiety. You see, you can not be relaxed and anxious at the same time. Physical and mental relaxation, like deep breathing, meditation, and muscle relaxation can help. I find that taking 15 minutes in the morning and 15 minutes at night to simply close my eyes and inhale to the count of 3 and exhale to the count of 5 helps me relax. It also has the added benefit of allowing me to clear my mind and then focus on my goals. It allows me to control my thoughts and cultivate a positive attitude.

**2. Learn to tolerate uncertainty** - It is important to accept. Uncertainty is part of life. Some people try to predict the future in an attempt to prevent unpleasant surprises and control the outcome. They focus on the worst case, but that does not make things turn out better.

**3. Identify and control your negative thoughts** - When something makes you worry, shift your focus. Start thinking about something pleasant. For me, shifting my focus does not help me to stop worrying for good. I find that the following tips work for me:

a. Write your worries down in a journal. This can help you to release them.

b. As worries come up, tell yourself you will worry about it later during your "worry time". Postponing your worrying helps you stop dwelling on your worries. Also, during this "worry time" you can review, examine and question your worries.

**4. Develop and maintain the right mental attitude** - Fill your mind with peace, hope and courage. Take time to be grateful every day and count your blessings. I find that shifting my focus to helping others allows me to forget my own challenges.

**Allow Lady Freedom to sum it all up.**

1. Worrying does not accomplish anything. Why worry? Do not worry. It is a waste of time.

2. Worrying can make you sick. Don't worry. It burdens your mind and body.

3. Worrying takes your focus on what really matters. Do not worry. Focus on what you are grateful for.

So, do not worry. Especially in difficult times like these, we need to control our thoughts, cultivate a positive mentality, and stay motivated. This will allow us to make positive changes in our lives.

**"Don't worry. Be happy."**

You can make it happen! So, do not worry about your business.

**Worry Is A Waste Of Time and Money.  Get Over It and Move On**

Worriers can find and create all sorts of things to worry about. People worry about:

The Economy

Their Health

Their Loved ones

Their Marriage

Making House Payments

Losing a Job

Gaining weight

The list goes on and on. Habitual worry creates diseases, divorces and disinterest in life.

Worry is not to be taken lightly. It is a serious contributor to poor mental and physical health and ineffective living.

When worries grown up they become anxiety, stress and suicidal thoughts.

If you are a worrier, you need to evaluate why and find ways to stop it.

What is worry?

Worry can be defined as nervously anticipating a future event or morbidly reliving a past event.

Worry is not reality. Worry is never about you're here and now. It never has to do with what is real in your life. It always has to do with the unreal chatter thoughts in your head.

You would do well to rid yourself of the habit of worry. Worrying is a habit and it can be broken. It wastes your valuable time, and it costs you money and life energy.

If you spent more time thinking constructive thoughts and concentrated on you're here and now instead of worrying about the past and the future; it's guaranteed, you'd:

Make more money.

Have more time

Have more fun

Enjoy more Peace of Mind

Worry has been defined as a state of being:

Worried

Concerned

Anxious

Troubled

Stressed

Uneasy

The truth of the matter is; It's never the issue that causes us problems. It is the worry, the concern over the issue.

The future and the past are two places you can't change. So why worry about them?

Glen Turner:
"Worry is like a rocking chair - - it gives you something to do but it doesn't get you anywhere."

Worry has also been defined as:

A strong feeling of anxiety

A sense of being troubled

A general uneasiness

A source of concern

It is a vague unpleasant emotion that is experienced in anticipation of some misfortune or a rehash of a past experience. Worry is never positive.

# Why people worry

Why do so many people spend so much time worrying?

Worrying is a good way to avoid taking personal responsibility.

Notice when you worry, it is about something or someone you think is causing you anxiety. You perceive the event or the person as the source of your unhappiness.

The first step to getting rid of worry is to see you as the cause of all your feelings. It is a fact, no one can make you feel anyway you don't want to feel.

If you're in a constant state of worry, you are:

Losing time

Losing money

Losing your peace of mind

Wasting your life
Stop It!

Unknown:
"Today is the tomorrow we worried about yesterday."

Worry is an emotion in which you feel anxious or concerned over an imagined issue. Common worry thoughts are about personal issues such as health, wealth, happiness, the future, the past, etc.

With real life issues, there is no time to worry.

People who are in charge of their life, seldom have time to worry.

Mark Twain:
"I am an old man and have known a great many troubles, but most of them never happened."

Many people are apprehensive when facing the unknown future. They tend to spend their time worrying rather than handling their present life situation.

Unknown:
"Blessed is the person who is too busy to worry in the daytime and too sleepy to worry at night."

Some people worry constantly, they worry:

At night

In the morning

Before and after appointments

In bed

In the car

Everywhere

They are constantly preoccupied with the future and the past

They are incapable of living in their present moment

Worriers are constantly thinking about unpleasant things that might happen. They refuse to accept that worry is never real.

Remember, worry is not a reality it is always a fantasy.

People who constantly worry are generally:

Afraid

Unhappy

Uneasy

Easily agitated

Robert Eliot:
" Rule number one is, don't sweat the small stuff. Rule number two is, it's all small stuff."

Summary

You can learn how to not worry. You can stop it. Today.

There are techniques and practices you can learn to help you stop worrying.

Once you're rid of worry, you're free to enjoy living with Peace of Mind.

**I really like this summary:**

**Mary C. Crowley:**
**"Every evening I turn my worries over to God. He's going to be up all night anyway."**

## Worry and Budgeting, A Formula For Heartburn

Some of the most frequently asked personal finance questions during any difficult economy revolve around "how to budget", "how to make a budget" and "how to live on a tight budget". Budgeting your money successfully is crucial to flourishing in any type of economy, much less a tough one. There is a common misconception that good budgeting depends upon fancy forms, financial expertise, software programs and solely on one's income. All of these false notions completely circumvent the only true goal of any personal budget: Getting the most value for each of your hard-earned dollars.

Those misguided beliefs above are the key reasons why many people are much worse off than they should be, regardless of income levels or familiarity with financial software. There are many people who are much "better off" with a lower income and a simple budget form than those with great salaries and top-notch computer programs. These successful folks are the ones who have learned the secret: Keenly stretch your dollars without sacrificing quality or "good living". This is the foundation for our budgeting method and it is the best method. It is the most effective method because it combines the three critical budgeting elements: Cost-cutting without sacrifice, timing your income/expenses and simple, accurate recordkeeping.

We have been successfully managing a household budget for nearly 30 years and have survived many unforeseen "bumps and bruises" along the way. During that time, we paid off our mortgage eight years early, sent two children through college, managed to save a good deal of money and maintained a nice standard of living. There were no magic tricks involved, just common sense, a few simple forms that we developed (see below) and a little effort. We have read countless "How to Budget" books and articles over the years and while a select few were beneficial, the majority we simply dismissed out of hand.

Unfortunately, most budget or personal finance "experts" approach cost-cutting from the standpoint of scaling back on items and niceties as a first choice, as opposed to a last resort, as it should be. One author for a popular financial web site even suggested eating a sandwich or a snack before going out to dinner because you would be less hungry and therefore saving some dollars. Taking this "logic" just a step further, why not just stay home and save even more? It is this type of lazy journalism and advice that keeps people meandering on the path to mediocrity. We had a good chuckle and moved on.

**There is a Better Way...**

The Dining Out Example:

The basic idea behind going out to dinner is to escape your stresses for a bit, have fun, relax, enjoy a change of scenery and forget about cooking and doing dishes for the evening. If you are going into it overly concerned about the financial aspect, you are nullifying the underlying relaxation intent. Our approach for "cutting back" on dining out expenses is quite the opposite: Cut only the bill, not the quality or quantity of dinner items. How so? By using Restaurant.com, anyone can cut their dining bill by 60% every day and up to 92% on special days. That is paying 8 cents on the dollar. This is a much more effective approach and no one needs to worry about filling up on pretzels on the way to the restaurant.

While well-intentioned, it is this narrow, defeatist assertion that we reject. Cutting back on products, services and enjoyment to save money is not getting ahead, it is trading off. And trading off is not the path to living better. We fully support frugality, with the added feature that you can be frugal AND attain a higher quality of living simultaneously. Certainly you shouldn't waste money on items which return little value but nor should you unnecessarily deprive yourself of the fruits of your labor. Break free from the antiquated "You can't have your cake and eat it too" crowd. A cake has only one purpose and the trick is to find the cheapest high-qality "baker".

It is this simple dining out example upon which our entire budgeting principle is based: Why spend more for something when you don't have to? We take it to an extreme however and raise the question to: Why spend MUCH more for something when you don't have to?

Much like visiting the local market and discovering that Joe is selling a bag of apples for 10 dollars while John is selling the same bag for 3 dollars, the choice is simple. in many cases, the "3 dollar apples" are of higher quality than those in the 10 dollar bag. This is the "secret" to getting ahead.

Our mindset and methodology on how to budget are clear:

1) Slash costs.
2) Maintain quality.
3) Pocket the difference.

The old adage is true: "A penny saved is a penny earned". The real goal though is to multiply the benefits of that adage over the course of time into "Thousands of dollars saved are thousands of dollars earned", while increasing your standard of living and net worth.

**How to Budget: Step by Step Instructions:**

**Step 1:** Find a quiet spot, relax, clear your mind and rid yourself of all of the over-complicated, force-fed convoluted advice that you have received over the years. Successful personal budgeting is easy and enjoyable, particularly the end result.

Gather all of your current information regarding income, debts, recurring expenses and discretionary (fun, entertainment) spending. This can be handwritten on a piece of scrap paper or with a collection of paystubs, bills, bank and credit card statements. To keep matters simple, use your after tax (net) income for purposes of using our forms. If you have savings, insurance or other expenses deducted from your paycheck, add those amounts back in to figure your net income. This will be your true net income, those "deducted" expenses will be listed in another area of your worksheet. Enter all of your data in the appropriate area of the Budget column on your Budget Form. This is a simple 3 column form with the headings: "Actual", "Budget" and "Variance". Do not be disheartened or discouraged if the results appear pessimistic at this point. Your only goal at this stage is to be certain that you have all of your items listed.

**Step 2:** This is the most critical and the most overlooked step by many people. It is the step which differentiates our plan from the majority of others which emphasize cutting your quality of life to save a buck.

Remember the theme: "Cut only your costs, not your enjoyment". This crucial area requires some upfront effort and will be well worth the time. In this step you will permanently cut the "fat" (overpaying) and this is the foundation upon which all of your future budgeting success depends. As you discover big savings on the payouts that you have already been making, this money will fall to the "bottom line", your pocket...where it belongs. Take your time and review the deals as well as any deals that you may find.

When you have good estimates for your cost-reduced budget figures, enter these figures in a New Budget column on a Comparison Shop Form. This is a simple 3 column form with the headings: "New Budget", "Original Budget" and "Variance". Enter the information from Step 1 in the Original Budget column and figure the variances. This will illustrate your newfound savings by category.

**Note:** This step may take some time before you have whittled down every one of your expense categories. Do not fret, use your best estimate at this point and adjust your figures as you move through later months. If you are in a dire hurry to get your budget done immediately, skip Steps 2 and 3 for now and revisit them later. Bear in mind the importance however, as this is the step which puts money back into your pocket.

**Step 3:** Adjust your budget and re-apply your newfound savings to some of your critical categories: Debt (particularly credit card debt), savings accounts and "fun" spending. These figures are entered in the New Budget column of the Budget Readjustment Form. This is a simple 3 column form with the headings: "New Budget", "Original Budget" and "Variance". Example: If you have been making only the minimum payments on your credit cards, increase these payments immediately for the sake of your long term financial health. Credit card interest is a killer and the longer these debts exist, the more damage it will do to your cash flow. Equally as important, comparison shop your current cards for better deals concerning interest rates and cash-back options. Enter your changes in the New Budget column. The goal here is to maintain virtually the same bottom line after you have readjusted your categories. These are now your official budget figures.

**Step 4:** At the conclusion of the first month, enter your actual spending in the Actual column of the Actual vs Budget Form and your newly budgeted figures in the Budget column of your form and figure your variances. This form is identical to the one in Step 1. This is your report of how well you performed for the month. Use this first month as your stepping stone for the future, with steady progress as your goal.

**Step 5:** This is the step that ties it all together: The Weekly Budget Form. This is a simple 3 column form with the headings: "Actual", "Budget" and "Variance", broken down by week. This form will be an immeasurable help in planning the timing of your bills and income. This form is completed much in the same manner as the others but is organized by week and due dates to ensure that your budgeting process will flow without any shortfalls in funds. Before the month begins, fill in all of your Budget data (according to your due dates) in the Budget column of the Weekly Budget Form.

The key here is to make certain that the figure labeled Gain or (Loss) for the month (at the bottom of your form) in the budget matches the figure labeled Balance in the budget column of your monthly Budget Form. It is imperative that these two figures are in sync before the month begins. At the completion of each week, fill in your actual data in the Actual column. When the month is complete, the actual and budget figures on the last line of the Weekly Budget Form should match the actual and budget figures on the last line of the Monthly Budget vs Actual Form. You will now have completed reports on a weekly and monthly basis for the month just ended.

**Guess what just happened:**

You just created a budget that will allow you to live comfortably but also within your means.  Talk about a stress buster/worry buster!  Now, doesn't that feel great?

# One Final Thought:

Each day as you get out of your nice warm bed and begin to prepare for what is before you STOP and say a simple prayer. It goes like this:

Dear Lord,

Please "give me this day my daily bread"

Yes, it is part of the Lord's Prayer. What is important to realize in this very short sentence of a prayer (you can and should expound on this as you worship) is that you are asking only for today's sustenance, nothing more. And that is as it should be. Yesterday has already taken place and there is very little you can actually do about tomorrow so would it not be best to just focus on today? Depend on the Creator, the one who gives you the breath you breathe each moment. Don't worry about what will happen. Rather remember also that it says in the Bible "Worry not. I provide for the birds and they have no home nor do they know where their next meal will come from. If I provide for the birds of the air would I not even more provide for you, my child?"

God bless you in your quest for peace and quiet tranquility in your life. In all things acknowledge Him and He will direct your paths.

www.ingramcontent.com/pod-product-compliance
Lightning Source LLC
Chambersburg PA
CBHW060815290526

45792CB00005BB/1660